THE PIANO BEN___
OF
CLASSICAL
MUSIC

AMSCO PUBLICATIONS
NEW YORK/LONDON/PARIS/SYDNEY/COPENHAGEN/MADRID

FOREWORD

For the classical pianist, the ideal piano bench should be sturdy, comfortable, and filled to the brim with the music of the great masters. The music books found within should provide many pathways through the world of piano literature—and reflect a range of musical periods, moods, and levels of difficulty.

This comprehensive volume provides the pianist with the ideal benchful of classical music. Here are the world's favorite inventions, preludes, and fugues of J.S. Bach; the beloved minuets and sonata movements of Scarlatti, Haydn, Mozart, and Beethoven; the exquisite nocturnes, waltzes, and intermezzos of Brahms and Chopin; the romantic short pieces of Schubert, Schumann, and Mendelssohn; and the sublime, impressionistic works of Debussy, Satie, and Scriabin.

This ideal classical piano bench should also include rewarding arrangements of great symphonic and chamber works. Within this volume, you will find favorite selections from the suites of Bach and Handel and themes from the great orchestral works of Haydn, Mendelssohn, Rimsky-Korsakov, and Mussorgsky, to name a few. For ballet and opera lovers, there are highlights from the masterworks of Bizet, Puccini, Rossini, Verdi, Tchaikovsky, and Wagner. For a bit of diversion, we have also included favorite light classics by Waldteufel, Ivanovici, and Strauss. To double the fun, there's even a selection of rewarding classical duets.

You hold in your hands enough piano music for a lifetime of playing pleasure and musical discovery. In this piano bench, you are sure to find many of your dearest old friends, and perhaps a few new ones.

COVER PHOTOGRAPH BACKGROUND: SUPERSTOCK
EDITOR: AMY APPLEBY
EDITORIAL ASSISTANT: DIANE TELFORD

ORDER NO. AM 961510
US INTERNATIONAL STANDARD BOOK NUMBER: 0.8256.1769.3
UK INTERNATIONAL STANDARD BOOK NUMBER: 0.7119.7900.6

EXCLUSIVE DISTRIBUTORS:
MUSIC SALES CORPORATION
257 PARK AVENUE SOUTH, NEW YORK, NY 10010 USA
MUSIC SALES LIMITED
8/9 FRITH STREET, LONDON W1V 5TZ ENGLAND
MUSIC SALES PTY. LIMITED
120 ROTHSCHILD STREET, ROSEBERY, SYDNEY, NSW 2018, AUSTRALIA

PRINTED IN THE UNITED STATES OF AMERICA BY
VICKS LITHOGRAPH AND PRINTING CORPORATION

THE PIANO BENCH OF CLASSICAL MUSIC

RENAISSANCE AND BAROQUE

CLASSICAL

ROMANTIC

IMPRESSIONIST AND MODERN

LIGHT CLASSICS

THEMES FROM THE OPERA

SCENES FROM THE BALLET

DUETS

Two-Part Invention No. 1

Johann Sebastian Bach
(1685–1750)

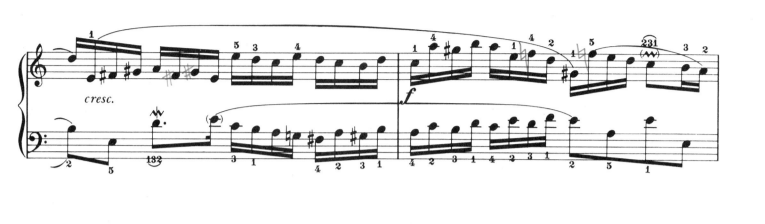

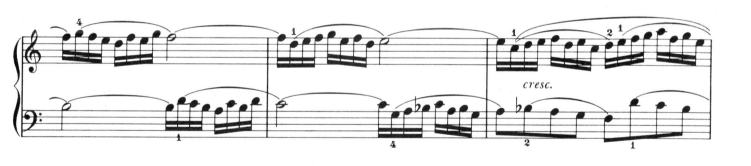

Two-Part Invention No. 4

Johann Sebastian Bach
(1685–1750)

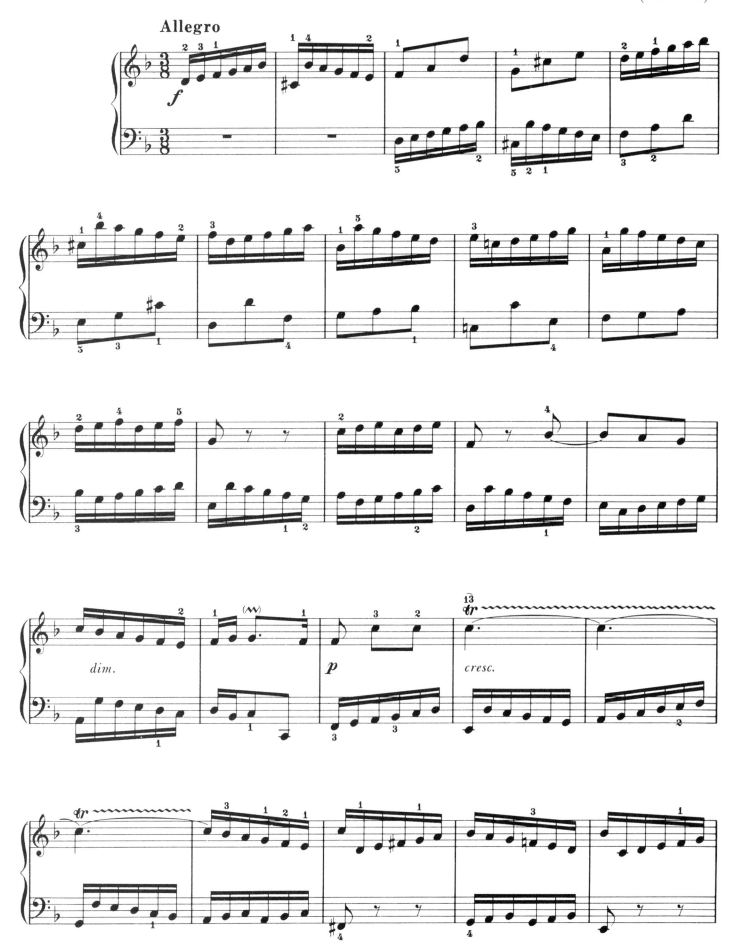

Two-Part Invention No. 8

Johann Sebastian Bach
(1685–1750)

Three-Part Invention No. 9

Johann Sebastian Bach
(1685–1750)

PRELUDE AND FUGUE IN C

from *The Well-Tempered Clavier*, Book 1, No. 1

Johann Sebastian Bach
(1685–1750)

Moderato

Andante

Chorale

Johann Sebastian Bach
(1685–1750)

SARABANDE
from *English Suite No. 1*

Johann Sebastian Bach
(1685–1750)

Loure
from *Third Cello Suite*

Johann Sebastian Bach
(1685–1750)

GAVOTTE
from *Sixth Cello Suite*

Johann Sebastian Bach
(1685–1750)

Allegro moderato

25

Fine

D.C. al Fine
senza reptizione

Bourée

from *Second Violin Sonata*

Johann Sebastian Bach
(1685–1750)

28

MINUET

Luigi Boccherini
(1743-1805)

TRIO

THE PRINCE OF DENMARK'S MARCH

from *Choice Lessons for the Harpsichord or Spinet*

Jeremiah Clarke
(1674-1707)

Les Tricoteuses
(The Knitters)

François Couperin
(1668-1733)

Bourée

George Frideric Handel
(1685–1759)

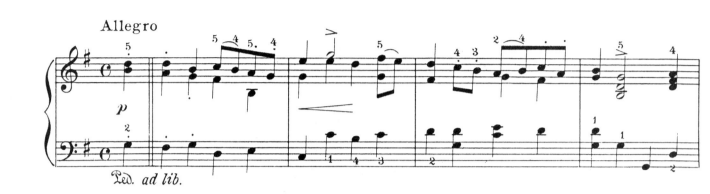

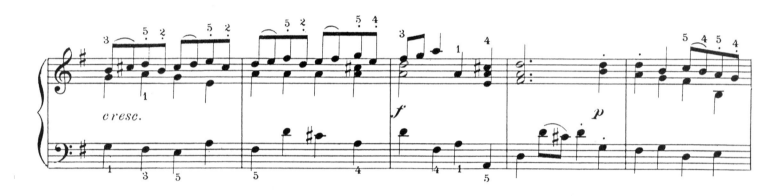

Sarabande

George Frideric Handel
(1685–1759)

THE HARMONIOUS BLACKSMITH

Air and Variations *Fifth Harpsichord Suite*

George Frideric Handel
(1685–1759)

Var. 2

Var. 3

legato

42

Var. 4

Var. 5

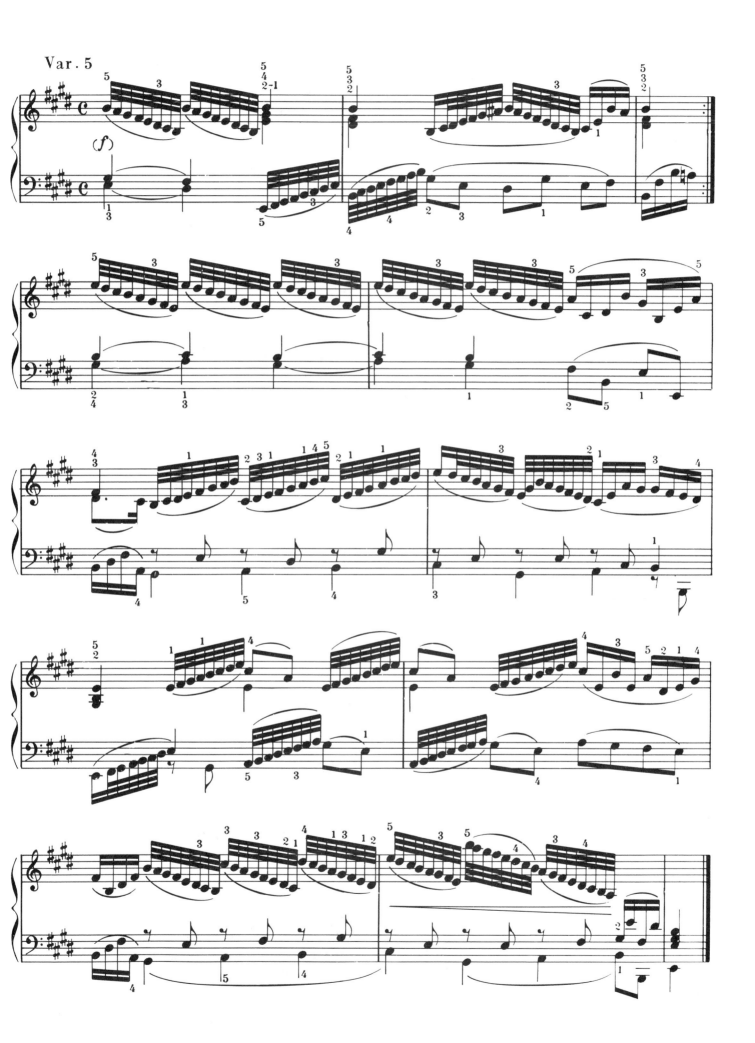

ALLEGRO
from *Suite No. 7*

George Frideric Handel
(1685–1759)

45

HALLELUJAH CHORUS
from *Messiah*

George Frideric Handel
(1685–1759)

Allegretto moderato

TRUMPET VOLUNTARY

Henry Purcell
(1659–1695)

Allegro moderato

SEE THE CONQUERING HERO COMES

from *Judas Maccabeus*

George Frideric Handel
(1685–1759)

GAVOTTE

Jean-Baptiste Lully
(1632-1687)

Allegro non troppo

Ped. ad lib.

MUSETTE

sempre legato

D.C. al Fine

MUSETTE EN RONDEAU

Jean-Philippe Rameau
(1683–1764)

Tempo di Ballo

Domenico Scarlatti
(1685–1757)

Sonata in D Minor

L. 313

Domenico Scarlatti
(1685–1757)

Allegro ♩ = 69

Rondo Espressivo

Carl Philipp Emanuel Bach
(1714-1788)

Andante sostenuto.

Für Elise

Ludwig van Beethoven
(1770–1827)

Poco moto

(Ped. simile)

Sonatina No. 1

Ludwig van Beethoven
(1770–1827)

Moderato

Romanza
Allegretto

SONATA IN G
Op. 49, No. 2

Ludwig van Beethoven
(1770–1827)

Allegro, ma non troppo

Tempo di Menuetto

ADAGIO

from *Moonlight Sonata*, Op. 27, No. 2

Ludwig van Beethoven
(1770–1827)

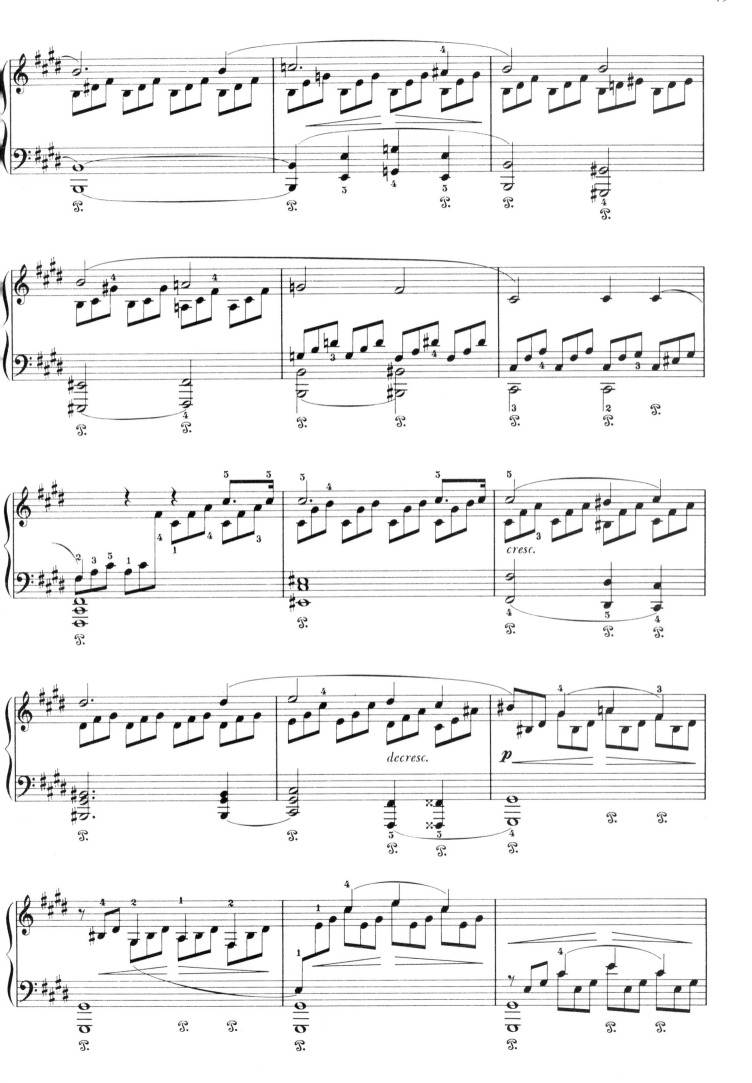

80

Allegro

from *Sonata in F Minor*, Op. 2, No. 1

Ludwig van Beethoven
(1770–1827)

84

Minuet in C

Ludwig van Beethoven
(1770–1827)

Trio

BAGATELLE IN C
Op. 119, No. 2

Ludwig van Beethoven
(1770–1827)

Andante con moto

THE GLORY OF GOD IN NATURE

Ludwig van Beethoven
(1770–1827)

Piano Sonata in C Minor

'Pathetique' Second Movement

Ludwig van Beethoven
(1770–1827)

Adagio cantabile

GAVOTTE

François Joseph Gossec
(1734-1829)

Minuet
from *Symphony in D*

Franz Joseph Haydn
(1732–1809)

Andante

from *'Surprise' Symphony*, No. 94

Franz Joseph Haydn
(1732–1809)

Maggiore

PIANO SONATA IN G

Hob. XVI:11

Franz Joseph Haydn
(1732–1809)

Da Capo (al 𝄐)

Menuet

Trio

Menuet da capo

GRAVE E CANTABILE

from *The Seven Last Words*

Franz Joseph Haydn
(1732–1809)

Serenade

Franz Joseph Haydn
(1732–1809)

Gigue in G
K.574

Wolfgang Amadeus Mozart
(1756–1791)

Minuet in D
K.355

Wolfgang Amadeus Mozart
(1756–1791)

ALLA TURCA

from *Sonata No. 11*, K. 331

Wolfgang Amadeus Mozart
(1756–1791)

MINUET

from *Divertimento No. 1*, K. 113

Wolfgang Amadeus Mozart
(1756–1791)

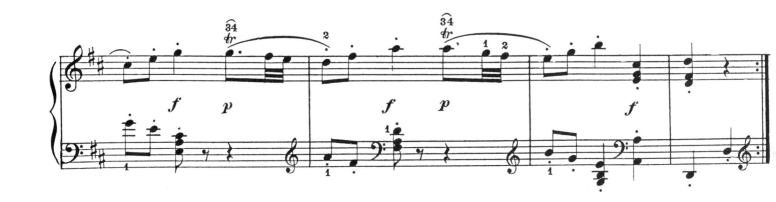

118

TRIO

D.C. al Fine

SONATA IN C
K.545

Wolfgang Amadeus Mozart
(1756–1791)

Allegro

Rondo （Allegro）

Intermezzo in A
Op. 118, No. 2

Johannes Brahms
(1833–1897)

Waltz in A-flat
Op. 39, No. 15

Johannes Brahms
(1833–1897)

PRELUDE IN E MINOR
Op. 28, No. 4

Frédéric Chopin
(1810–1849)

Largo

WALTZ IN C-SHARP MINOR
Op. 64, No. 2

Frédéric Chopin
(1810–1849)

142

WALTZ IN A-FLAT
Op. 69, No. 1

Frédéric Chopin
(1810–1849)

146

Nocturne in E-flat
Op. 9, No. 2

Frédéric Chopin
(1810–1849)

Mazurka in C
Op. 67, No. 3

Frédéric Chopin
(1810–1849)

Nocturne No. 5

John Field
(1782–1837)

Cantabile, assai lento

Nocturne
Op. 54, No. 4

Edvard Grieg
(1843–1907)

Tempo I

CONSOLATION
No. 5 from *Six Consolations*

Franz Liszt
(1811–1886)

LIEBESTRAUM

No. 3 from *Three Notturnos*

Franz Liszt
(1811–1886)

Poco allegro, con affetto

dolce cantando

Confidence
Op. 19, No. 4

Felix Mendelssohn
(1809–1847)

Spring Song
Op. 62, No. 6

Felix Mendelssohn
(1809–1847)

Allegretto grazioso

Capriccio in A

Op. 16, No. 1

Felix Mendelssohn
(1809–1847)

Andante con moto

173

174

poco ritard. sin' al ... ... tempo dell' Andante

Wedding March

from *A Midsummer Night's Dream*

Felix Mendelssohn
(1809–1847)

Spinning Song
Op. 67, No. 4

Felix Mendelssohn
(1809–1847)

182

Serenade
Op. 90, No. 11

Franz Schubert
(1797–1828)

MOMENT MUSICALE
Op. 94, No. 3

Franz Schubert
(1797–1828)

Allegro moderato

(staccato sempre)

Scherzo in B-flat

Franz Schubert
(1797–1828)

Trio

Scherzo D.C.

AVE MARIA

Franz Schubert
(1797–1828)

Impromptu in A-flat
Op. 142, No. 2

Franz Schubert
(1797–1828)

Schlummerlied

Robert Schumann
(1810–1856)

REMEMBRANCE
Op. 68, No. 28

Robert Schumann
(1810–1856)

Träumerei
Op. 15, No. 7

Robert Schumann
(1810–1856)

Why?
Op. 12, No. 3

Robert Schumann
(1810–1856)

Langsam und zart
Lento e suave (♩ = 56)

SONATA

First and Second Movements, Op. 118, No. 1

Robert Schumann
(1810–1856)

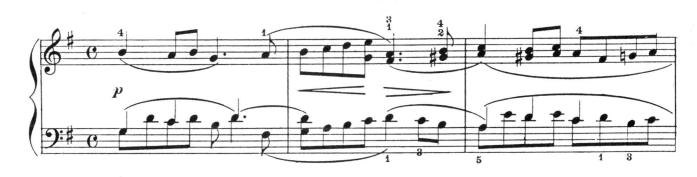

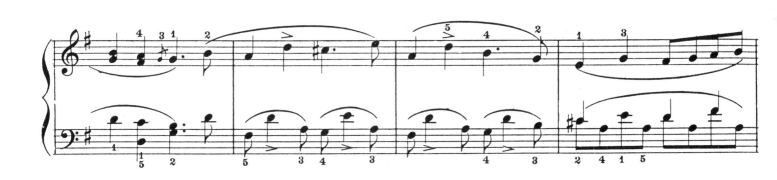

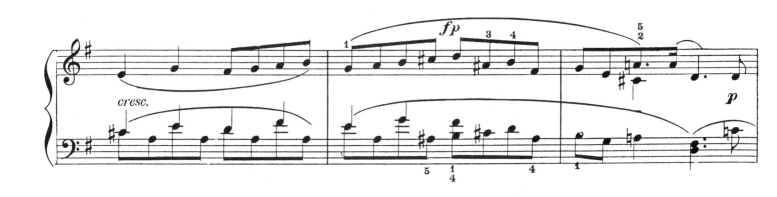

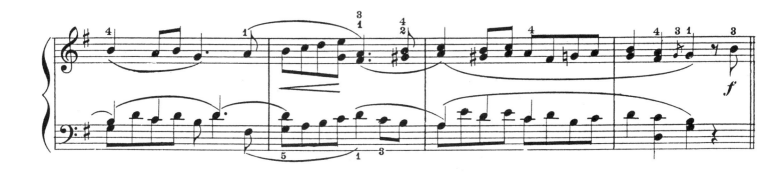

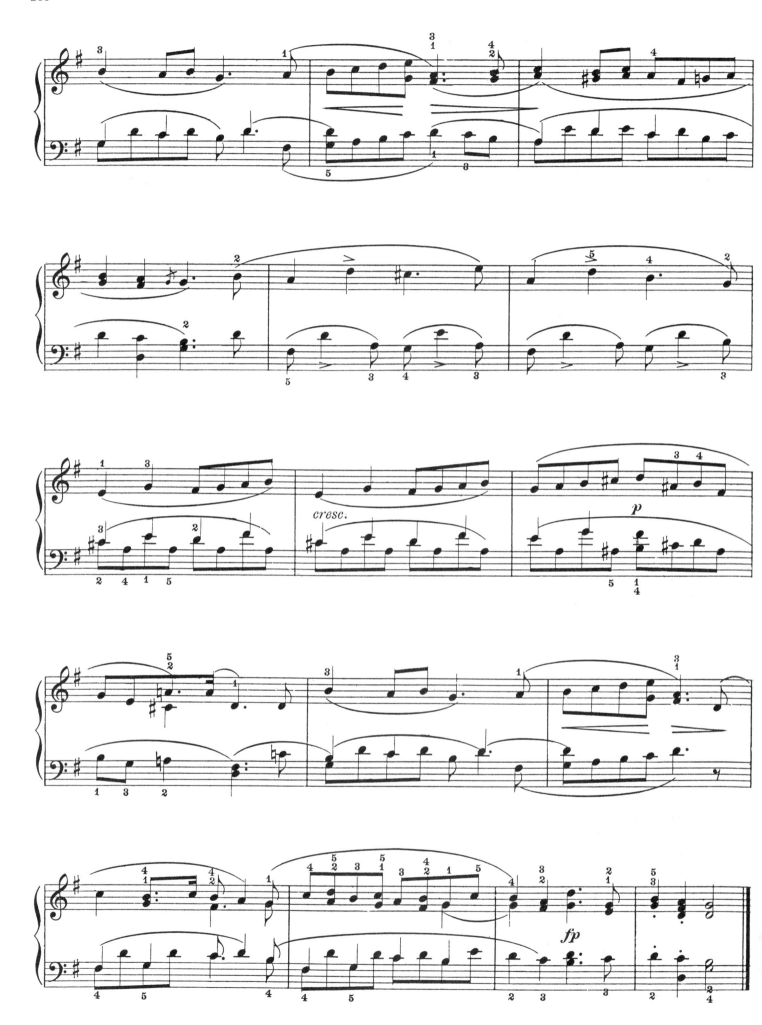

Chanson Triste
Op. 40, No. 2

Peter Ilyich Tchaikovsky
(1840–1893)

Allegro non troppo
la melodia con molto espressione

WALTZ
Op. 39, No. 8

Peter Ilyich Tchaikovsky
(1840–1893)

TANGO

Isaac Albéniz
(1860–1909)

MINSTRELS
from *Preludes,* Book 1

Claude Debussy
(1862–1918)

LA FILLE AUX CHEVEUX DE LIN

'The Girl with the Flaxen Hair' from *Preludes,* Book 1

Claude Debussy
(1862–1918)

CLAIR DE LUNE
'Moonlight' from *Suite Bergamasque*

Claude Debussy
(1862–1918)

Andante très expressif

HUMORESQUE
Op. 101, No. 7

Antonín Dvořák
(1841–1904)

VALSES POETICOS No. 2

Enrique Granados
(1867–1916)

To a Wild Rose
Op. 51, No. 1

Edward MacDowell
(1860–1908)

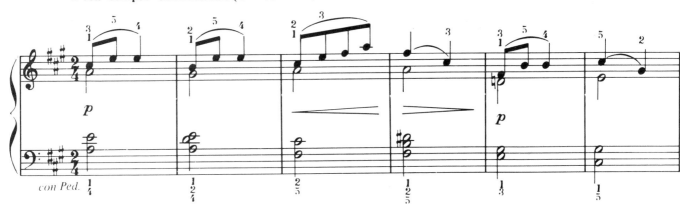

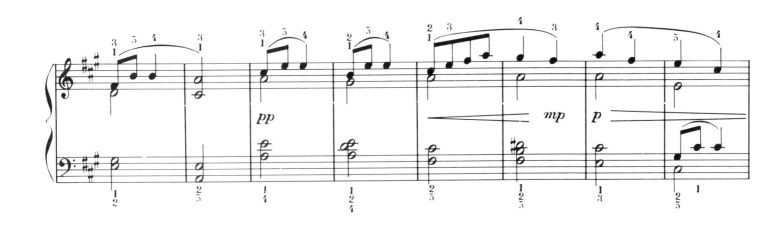

ELEGIE
Op. 10

Jules Massenet
(1842–1912)

Lento, ma non troppo

(con espressione)

BYDLO

'The Oxcart' from *Pictures at an Exhibition*

Modeste Mussorgsky
(1839–1881)

The Young Prince and the Young Princess

from *Scheherezade*, Op. 35

Nikolai Rimsky-Korsakov
(1844–1908)

Andantino, quasi allegretto

ROMANCE
Op. 44

Anton Rubinstein
(1829–1894)

Trois Gymnopédies

Erik Satie
(1866–1925)

1

Lent et douloureux

2

Lent et triste

3

Prelude in A Minor
Op. 11, No. 2

Alexander Scriabin
(1872–1915)

Album Leaf
Op. 45, No. 1

Alexander Scriabin
(1872–1915)

SIMPLE AVEU

François Thomé
(1850-1909)

Prelude in D
Op. 11, No. 5

Alexander Scriabin
(1872–1915)

Entry of the Gladiators

Julius Fučik
(1872–1916)

Tempo di Marcia

Trio

Octava ad lib

La Cinquantaine
(The Golden Wedding)

Gabriel-Marie

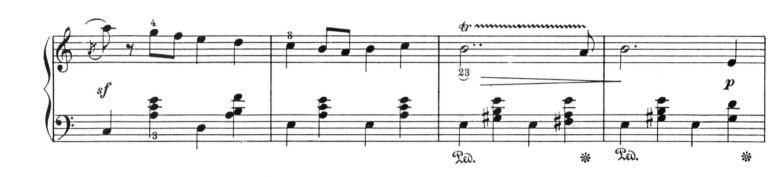

Le Secret

Leonard Gautier

270

FUNERAL MARCH OF A MARIONETTE

Charles Gounod
(1818–1893)

274

DANUBE WAVES

Iosif Ivanovici
(c.1845–1902)

2.

278

4.

D.S. al Fine

OVER THE WAVES

Juventino Rosas

282

One Heart, One Mind

Johann Strauss
(1825–1899)

Trio

D.C. ad lib.

Blue Danube Waltz

Johann Strauss
(1825–1899)

D. C. ad lib. al 𝄐

Skaters Waltz

Emil Waldteufel
(1837–1915)

Tempo di Valse

294

La Paloma

Sebastian Yradier
(1809–1865)

CARMEN
(Themes)

Georges Bizet
(1838–1875)

Con moto (Toreador Song)

con Ped.

302

Tempo di Marcia

ben macato

con Ped.

(Toreador's March)

brillante

Ped.   simile

FAUST
(Themes)

Charles Gounod
(1818–1893)

Tempo di Marcia (Soldiers' Chorus)

Mouvement de Valse (Waltz)

Allegretto (Flower Song)

Andante (Love Duet)

309

Adagio (Duet "O Moonlight")

Moderato maestoso ("Angels Rare, Angels Radiant")

THE MARRIAGE OF FIGARO
(Themes)

Wolfgang Amadeus Mozart
(1756–1791)

Andante (You Who Love's Power)

Allegro moderato (Sweet Ladies)

314

TALES OF HOFFMAN
(Themes)

Jacques Offenbach
(1819–1880)

318

Allegro Moderato

Ped. ✳

(Student's Chorus)

con Ped. ad lib.

La Bohème
(Musetta's Waltz)

Giacomo Puccini
(1858–1924)

WILLIAM TELL
(Themes)

Gioacchino Antonio Rossini
(1792–1868)

Andante (Overture)

Allegretto (Ballet Music)

Die Fledermaus
(Themes)

Johann Strauss
(1825–1899)

Moderato con moto (Such a fine gentleman)

con Ped. ad lib.

poco string.

ritard.

a tempo

Tempo di Valse (Waltz)

(Ah, what a Feast, what a Night of Joy)

H.M.S. Pinafore
(Themes)

Arthur Sullivan
(1842–1900)

Allegro (We sail the Ocean Blue)

Andante (Sorry her Lot)

Poco animato

cresc.

f

Ped. ✳ Ped. ✳ Ped. ✳

Allegretto (Im called little Buttercup)

p

Ped. ✳ Ped. ✳ Ped. ✳ Ped. simile

Allegretto (I am the Captain of the "Pinafore")

Maestoso (For he is an Englishman)

AIDA
(Themes)

Giuseppe Verdi
(1813–1901)

Andantino (Heav'nly Aïda)

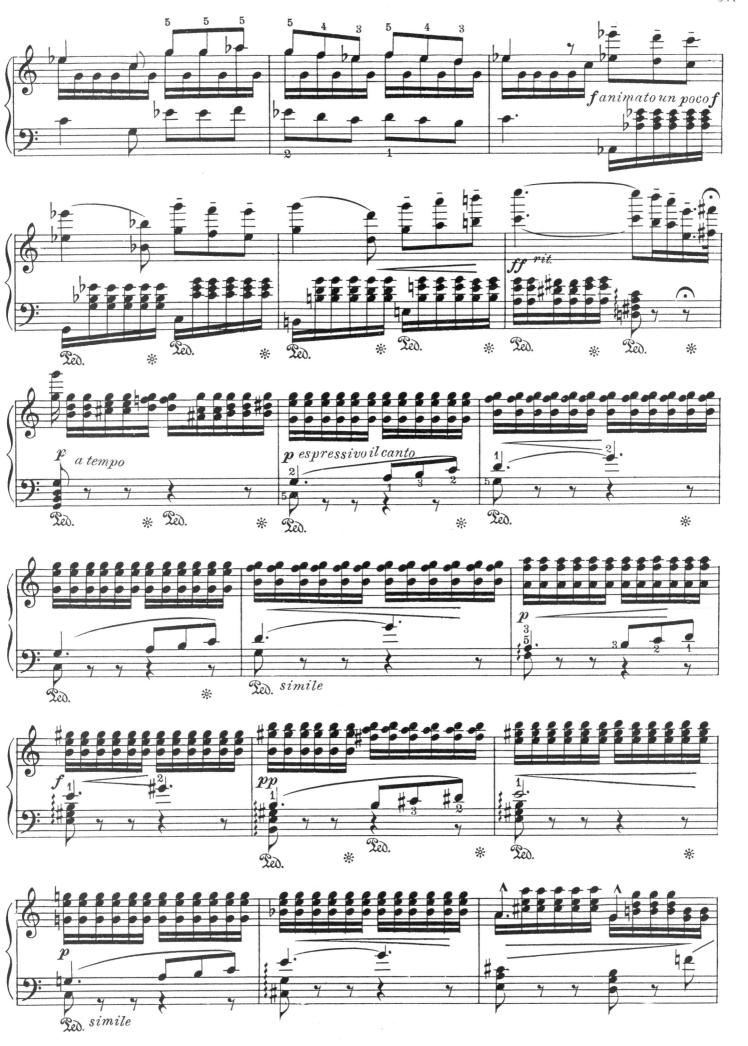

Allegro animato

Allegro moderato (Triumphal March)

LOHENGRIN
(Bridal Chorus)

Richard Wagner
(1813–1883)

VALSE LENTE
from *Coppélia*

Léo Delibes
(1836–1891)

PIZZICATO

from *Sylvia*

Léo Delibes
(1836–1891)

Allegretto ben moderato

Aragonaise

from *Le Cid*

Jules Massenet
(1842–1912)

357

Dance of the Hours
from *La Gioconda*

Amilcare Ponchielli
(1834–1886)

Moderato

ENTR'ACTE

from *Rosamunde*

Franz Schubert
(1797–1828)

Andantino

MINORE

LOVE THEME

from *Romeo and Juliet*

Peter Ilyich Tchaikovsky
(1840–1893)

Moderato

cresc. poco a poco

mf

dim.

p

DANCE OF THE SUGAR PLUM FAIRY

from *The Nutcracker*

Peter Ilyich Tchaikovsky
(1840–1893)

DANCE OF THE REED FLUTES

from *The Nutcracker*

Peter Ilyich Tchaikovsky
(1840–1893)

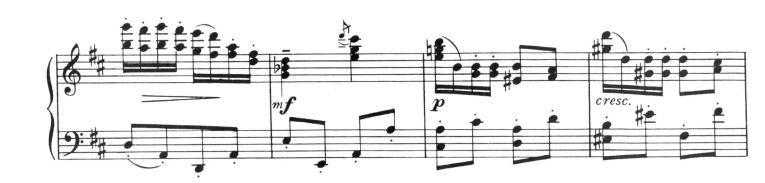

con espressione

RUSSIAN DANCE
from *The Nutcracker*

Peter Ilyich Tchaikovsky
(1840–1893)

Molto vivace

WALTZ
from *Sleeping Beauty*

Peter Ilyich Tchaikovsky
(1840–1893)

Tempo di valse

Minuet in G

Ludwig van Beethoven
(1770–1827)

Secondo

Minuet in G

Ludwig van Beethoven
(1770–1827)

Primo

Waltz

Johannes Brahms
(1833–1897)

Secondo

WALTZ

Johannes Brahms
(1833–1897)

Primo

Prelude

Frédéric Chopin
(1810–1849)

Secondo

Andante Rubato

PRELUDE

Frédéric Chopin
(1810–1849)

Primo

Polonaise

Antonio Diabelli
(1781–1858)

Secondo

Polonaise

Antonio Diabelli
(1781–1858)

Primo

Allegretto

Consolation

Secondo

Felix Mendelssohn
(1809–1847)

Consolation

Felix Mendelssohn
(1809–1847)

Primo

TWO GERMAN DANCES

Franz Schubert
(1797–1828)

Secondo

TWO GERMAN DANCES

Franz Schubert
(1797–1828)

Primo

Chant sans Paroles

Peter Ilyich Tchaikovsky
(1840–1893)

Secondo

Allegretto grazioso e cantabile

CHANT SANS PAROLES

Peter Ilyich Tchaikovsky
(1840–1893)

Primo

Secondo

Primo